I.   Introduction

Although researchers have made innumerable attempts to analyze the relationship between competition (as proxied by concentration) and performance (*e.g.*, price), empirical evidence on the actual competitive effects of horizontal mergers is scarce. Perhaps this is not surprising. When assessed by contemporary antitrust standards, most mergers (even most horizontal mergers) do not present a serious risk of competitive harm. The handful that do typically either will be blocked in their entirety, or approved conditional on the completion of some remedial action (*e.g.*, the divestiture of a critical competitive asset to a third party) designed to ameliorate the risk of competitive harm. Hence, candidates for the study of (plausibly) anticompetitive mergers will arise only infrequently; when, for example, the enforcement agencies lose a merger challenge in court, obtaining no competitive relief, or when the enforcement agencies do not challenge a transaction for reasons unrelated to the transaction's perceived competitive effects.

This paper takes advantage of one of these rare opportunities. We provide an econometric analysis of a horizontal merger in a concentrated hospital market, Dominican Santa Cruz Hospital's acquisition of its sole rival in the city of Santa Cruz, California, AMI-Community Hospital. According to the FTC, only two competitors -- both not-for-profit -- remained in the relevant market after the transaction.[1] Absent substantial efficiencies, or a credible threat of entry, standard antitrust analysis would predict that an increase in concentration of this magnitude likely would lead to higher

---

[1] *See* Complaint *In the Matter of Santa Cruz Hospital, et al.* 188 F.T.C. 382 (1994).

equilibrium prices. Consequently, this transaction would have been challenged by the FTC, had the Commission been able to intervene before the transaction was completed.[2] However, because the transaction was too small (in absolute size) to trigger the Hart-Scott-Rodino filing thresholds, the FTC did not receive prior notification of the transaction, and the parties were able to consummate the acquisition before the FTC could seek a preliminary injunction. Ultimately, the FTC entered into a consent order with Dominican Hospital, but the decree required only that Dominican notify the Commission prior to any further acquisitions in the relevant geographic market – it did not restore the premerger market structure. For this reason, this acquisition provides an excellent opportunity to assess, *ex post*, the actual, as opposed to the predicted, competitive consequences of a horizontal merger.

This study should be of interest for at least two reasons. First, as noted, empirical studies of the price effects of horizontal mergers are comparatively rare, notwithstanding their apparent importance to appraising the efficacy of federal merger enforcement policy. Studies such as this should help policymakers assess whether the enforcement decision rules embodied in the *Merger Guidelines* predict with an acceptable degree of accuracy the competitive consequences of actual horizontal mergers.

---

[2] *See* Statement of Chairman Janet D. Steiger in Support of Final Issuance of Consent Order *In the Matter of Dominican Santa Cruz Hospital, et al.* 188 F.T.C. 382 (1994).

Second, and more specifically, the applicability to hospital markets of the antitrust agencies' approach to horizontal merger analysis (*i.e.,* the *Merger Guidelines*) recently has been called into question. A substantial share of hospital output (approximately 90 percent) is produced by private and public nonprofit hospitals. Critics have contended that the antitrust agencies and courts have assumed that these not-for-profit providers seek maximum profits, notwithstanding the substantial body of theoretical and empirical analyses suggesting that nonprofit entities -- or more specifically, certain types of nonprofit entities -- will eschew opportunities to profitably exercise market power.[3] For example (see Lynk (1995), pp. 440-41), it is conceivable that a private nonprofit hospital sponsored and administered by the local community, might function something like a consumer cooperative. If so, the incentives of producers and consumers would be aligned, and any incentives the hospital might otherwise have to raise prices anticompetitively would be attenuated. Alternatively, the behavior of a nonprofit hospital whose profits are used to fund some particular set of activities valued the firm's managers – *e.g.,* providing charity care to the poor – might be indistinguishable from that of an identically situated for-profit entity.

Whether the (potentially) different incentive structure of not-for-profit hospitals could attenuate the exercise of market power is of more than just academic interest. The courts that must adjudicate horizontal merger challenges also have found such

---

[3] *See* Lynk (1994, 1995) for a more detailed review of the relevant theory and evidence.

arguments compelling. In at least one case,[4] a U.S. Federal District Court found that the nonprofit, community-sponsored status of the merging parties was an important factor in rebutting an otherwise convincing *prima facie* case against the merger of two rival hospitals.

The transaction analyzed here provides an excellent opportunity to explore these possibilities. The acquiring entity (Dominican Santa Cruz Hospital) is part of a chain of Catholic hospitals operating in the western United States. Its sole remaining rival in Santa Cruz county, Watsonville Community, is a locally-sponsored community hospital. According to the arguments set forth above, Watsonville Community would appear to be the type of nonprofit hospital least prone to exercise market power; any such propensity to charge competitive prices would, moreover, place a powerful post-merger competitive constraint on Dominican's ability to raise prices. Consequently, an analysis of both entities' (but especially Watsonville's) post-merger pricing behavior should provide a valuable insight into the behavior of nonprofit producers.

The next section reviews briefly the empirical literature on hospital competition. We review first those studies that have explored the empirical relationship between concentration and hospital prices. These studies for the most part are cross-sectional in nature, and do not specifically investigate the equilibrium effects of actual horizontal

---

[4] *See F.T.C. v. Butterworth Health Corporation and Blodgett Memorial Medical Center,* (U.S. District Court, Western District of Michigan, Southern Division), September 26, 1996, slip. op. at 27.

mergers. The effects of mergers (including hospital mergers) are the focus of the second, much smaller (but much more recent) body of research that we review.

Section III describes briefly the details of the Dominican-Santa Cruz transaction. Section IV outlines the empirical strategy for studying the price effects of that merger. Section V presents the empirical results.

II. Studies of Hospital Competition

A. Cross Sectional Studies

Most early (*i.e.,* pre-1983[5]) studies of hospital competition were carried out using a variant of the well-known "Structure-Conduct-Performance" (S-C-P) paradigm. As noted by Bresnahan (1989, pp. 1012-13), the distinguishing features of this empirical paradigm are reflected in the following assumptions: first, that price-cost margins can be accurately measured with accounting data; and second, that cross-sectional variation in market structure can be measured with a small number of observable variables (including market concentration). Early studies of hospital competition varied the standard SCP approach slightly by assuming that hospitals engaged mainly in quality, rather than price, competition. Accordingly, the typical study from this period attempted to discern the relationship between some measure of hospital *costs* (*e.g.,* cost

---

[5] The year 1983 is significant in most analyses of hospital markets because this is the year Medicare instituted the prospective payment system (PPS). It is also the year in which California enacted legislation permitting selective contracting between health plans and individual hospitals.

per admission) to some measure of competition.[6] Usually, a *negative* relationship

between hospital concentration and costs was found (*e.g.,* higher costs per admission

were observed in the less concentrated markets).[7] Generally, this finding was

interpreted as reflecting the consequences of insurance-induced moral hazard, and

other principal-agent problems.

Studies using data from the mid-1980s and after, and which focus on the

California experience, present a different picture. Typically, these studies addressed

the relationship between market concentration and *price*, as opposed to market

structure and *cost*, and generally, they obtained results consistent with the traditional S-

C-P paradigm -- *i.e.,* a *positive* relationship between concentration and price.[8]

While suggestive, these price-concentration studies do not provide direct

evidence of the effects of hospital mergers. One problem with drawing inferences about

the competitive effects of mergers from this literature is that the results are almost

surely sensitive to the way the geographic markets are defined, since this definition will

---

[6] A notable exception was Noether (1988), who found that increased competition reduced mark-ups over cost.

[7] For a comprehensive review of this literature see Pautler and Vita (1994). For seminal works see Joskow (1980) and Robinson and Luft (1985).

[8] For example, Dranove *et al.* (1993) found that an increase in the Herfindahl-Hirschman Index (HHI) from 2500 to 5000 results in a price increase of approximately 3 percent for a basket of hospital services. Melnick *et al.* (1992) found that where a merger reduces the number of competitors from three to two (assuming that the competitors had equal shares), the per diem price for medical/surgical services increases by 9 percent. Other examples are Keeler, Melnick, and Zwanziger (1999), and Simpson and Shin (1998).

determine the value of the concentration index.   Most of these studies delineated

markets with political boundaries (*e.g.,* counties or MSAs), although some have

attempted to use patient origin data to define markets (*e.g.,* Melnick *et al.* (1992)). Even

the latter approach, while seemingly less arbitrary than using political boundaries, has

been criticized as presenting biased view of actual antitrust markets.[9]   The second

problem is more fundamental, and derives from the disfavor into which the S-C-P

approach has fallen. Although studies continue to be carried out in this paradigm,

many economists have grown skeptical about the validity of its maintained hypotheses

-- in particular, the notion that cross-sectional variation in prices can be explained with

a small number of observable variables (*see* Bresnahan (1989, pp. 1012-13).

Consequently, alternative approaches to identifying and measuring market power have

been derived. In the following section, we discuss one such approach that has been

adopted as a means for assessing the competitive consequences of horizontal mergers.

---

[9] For example, see Kessler and McClellan (1999) and Werden (1989). Only the former have offered an alternative method for defining antitrust markets. Although there seldom may be good practical alternatives to patient flow data, it is nonetheless true that antitrust markets defined on this basis may lead to incorrect conclusions about the competitive constraints faced by a particular pair of merging hospitals.

B. Empirical Literature on Actual Mergers

An alternative strategy to the S-C-P paradigm for assessing the equilibrium consequences of merger-induced changes in market structure is to examine directly, through a comparison of the pre- and post-merger prices charged by the merged entity (and, perhaps, its plausible rivals), the equilibrium effects of the transaction. This "event study" approach obviates the necessity of defining the "relevant market."[10] If the merger creates market power, then (after suitably controlling for other possible shifts in the exogenous determinants of price) one should observe the merged entity raising its price post-merger. It is unnecessary to identify the relevant market to carry out this test -- at minimum, one requires only data for the merged entity.[11]

_____

[10] Another form of "event study" sometimes used by economists are stock market event studies, which examine the effect of an event (*e.g.,* the announcement of a merger) on the stock market value of some set of affected firms (*e.g.,* rivals of the merging entities). *See* MacKinlay (1997) for a general description of this approach. The stock market event study method on a number of occasions has been used to assess the consequences of horizontal mergers (*see, e.g.,* Eckbo (1983)), and we are aware of at least one attempt to use this method to evaluate the competitive consequences of hospital mergers (Woolley (1989); *see* Vita and Schumann (1991) for a critique of this study). While the stock market event study method applied to horizontal merger analysis does not require the researcher to identify the precise boundaries of the antitrust market, it does require the researcher to identify at least some of the firms whose profits likely would be affected by the transaction.

[11] Of course, one can do more. In the empirical section below, we also estimate the effects of the merger on the price of (what appears to be) the merged entity's closest rival. Failure to find a positive price effect for this producer might mean either that this firm (1) did not produce a close substitute; or (2) the merger did not create market power. Finding a positive price effect would suggest (*ceteris paribus*) that the producer

(continued...)

Among the first researchers to employ this strategy were Barton and Sherman (1984), who found that two mergers of microfilm producers increased both prices and profits. A very similar empirical strategy was used by Kim and Singal (1993) in their study of the price effects of airline mergers. Later, Schumann *et al.* (1992, 1997) examined the price effects of mergers that took place in three different industries: cement, corrugated paperboard, and titanium dioxide.[12]

Barton and Sherman, and Kim and Singal used a very simple -- and restrictive -- empirical strategy for measuring the competitive impact of a horizontal merger. Essentially, they analyzed movements in the price of the product affected by the merger, relative to the price of a substitute product hypothesized to face similar demand and cost conditions, but unaffected (or at least less affected) by the merger. The competitive effects of the transaction were assessed through a simple t-test of the

---

[11] (...continued)
was in the relevant market, and that the merger was anticompetitive.

[12] Connor, Feldman, and Dowd (1998), and Wicks, Meyer, and Carlyn (1998) also attempted to assess the price effects of horizontal hospital mergers, but both studies exhibit considerable methodological problems. Connor *et al.* estimate an equation of the form: $\%? \text{PRICE}_{it} = f(\%? X_{it}, M_i)$, where the dependent variable is the percentage change price of the ith hospital from period $t\text{-}1$ to period t, X_{it} are exogenous variables, and M_i is a dummy variable set equal to 1 if hospital i merged during the sample period. It is difficult to reconcile this specification with economic theory, which predicts a relationship between the price *level* (not its rate-of-change) and market structure. Additionally, it appears that the merger dummy variable is either 0 or 1 for the entire sample period, instead of taking on different values for the pre- and post-merger periods.

Wicks *et al.* (1998) compare pre- and post-merger price levels, but do not include any control variables. Hence, it is difficult to know if any changes in prices reflect the exercise of market power, or are the result of changes in exogenous price determinants.

hypothesis that the pre-merger price ratio equaled the post-merger ratio, against the alternative that the ratio increased. No other control variables were employed in the analysis – the authors assumed, implicitly, that the reduced form price equations for both products were identical, and therefore that the differences in the ratios of the prices could be attributed solely to changes in market structure.[13]

Schumann *et al.* (1992, 1997) adopted a different approach – they estimated a reduced form price equation with data spanning the pre- and post-merger periods.[14] The competitive effect of the transaction was captured with a dummy variable set equal to one for the post-merger period. By using this specification, Schumann *et al.* assume that their control variables (consisting mainly of indices of demand and factor prices) adequately control for the exogenous determinants of price, so that the coefficient on the merger dummy variable can be interpreted as reflecting the competitive effects of the transaction. If, however, there are unobserved exogenous determinants of price that are correlated with the merger dummy, then the coefficient on this variable will reflect the competitive effects of the transaction, as well as movements in these unobserved

---

[13] Kim and Singal (1993, p. 554) rationalize this as follows: "Industry-wide changes, like fluctuations in fuel prices, changes in labor cost, and seasonal or cyclical variations in demand are likely to have an equivalent effect on routes of a similar distance." They go on to observe (footnote 20): "Local economic conditions may affect some routes differently. We hope the large number of observations in our sample averages out the noise."

[14] By "reduced form," we mean that they regressed price on its exogenous determinants (*e.g.*, demand- and cost-shifters).

price determinants. As a consequence, one will incorrectly estimate the price effects of the transaction.

In the empirical section below, we propose an empirical framework that combines elements of the Barton and Sherman, and Schumann *et al.* approaches. We believe that this strategy will provide the best method for identifying accurately the competitive effects of the acquisition. Before setting forth this empirical strategy, we first describe in greater detail the events of the Dominican-Santa Cruz transaction.

III.   **History of the Transaction**

On March 8, 1990, Dominican Santa Cruz Hospital ("Dominican"), a 259-bed, not-for-profit hospital, affiliated with the Catholic Healthcare West system, purchased the only other hospital in the city of Santa Cruz, AMI-Community Hospital ("Community"). Community, which was affiliated with American Medical International, was licensed for 180 beds and was a for-profit entity. Dominican and Community were located about two miles apart. The only other hospital in Santa Cruz county was Watsonville Community Hospital, located about 14 miles south of the city. The city of Santa Cruz is located about 40 miles south of San Jose, and 80 miles south of San Francisco. Santa Cruz county is bordered on the south and west by the Pacific ocean, and on the north and east by the Santa Cruz mountains.

The FTC's analysis of patient flows suggested that the overwhelming majority of the three Santa Cruz county hospitals' patients resided in Santa Cruz county, and that most Santa Cruz residents receiving inpatient hospital care received it from hospitals in the county. Accordingly, the FTC's complaint alleged that the relevant geographic market was "Santa Cruz County and/or portions of Santa Cruz County." According to the Complaint, the merger increased the market share (of patient-days) of Dominican from 62 percent to approximately 73 percent, and increased the market share (measured by available beds) from 50 percent to 73 percent. The Herfindahl-Hirschman Index for the relevant antitrust market increased by over 1,700 points, from approximately 4,620 to approximately 6,350 (measured by patient-days); and by over 2,300 points (from approximately 3,770 to approximately 6,090) when measured by available beds. Under the *Merger Guidelines* enforcement criteria, a transaction generating concentration figures of this magnitude would be presumed anticompetitive. Absent compelling evidence that such a merger would create substantial efficiencies, or that the exercise of market power would be constrained by the threat of entry, normally the FTC would seek to preliminarily enjoin such a transaction.[15] Had the FTC had the opportunity to seek a preliminary injunction in this case, it would have done so.[16] However, as noted

---

[15] According to the 1992 *Merger Guidelines* (§1.51(c)), "the [FTC] regards markets [with HHIs above 1800] to be highly concentrated . . . [when] the post-merger HHI exceeds 1800, it will be presumed that mergers producing an increase in the HHI of more than 100 points are likely to create or enhance market power or facilitate its exercise."

[16] As then-FTC Chairman Steiger observed at the time, "[t]he facts of this case provide sufficient reason to believe that this acquisition violates Section 7 of the Clayton Act. Ordinarily, such facts would lead the Commission to seek a preliminary injunction in federal district court." *See* Statement of Chairman Janet D. Steiger in Support of Final
(continued...)

earlier, the small absolute size of the transaction failed to trigger the Hart-Scott-Rodino filing thresholds, and the FTC was not able to seek an enforcement action until after the transaction was completed.

In March, 1993, approximately three years after the merger was consummated, the FTC accepted a consent agreement with Dominican Santa Cruz Hospital and Catholic Healthcare West. The consent order did nothing to restore the pre-merger competitive environment; it required only that the respondents obtain the Commission's prior approval before acquiring any other hospitals in Santa Cruz County. Although all of the FTC Commissioners concluded that the merger probably had created significant market power, a majority of the FTC Commissioners concluded that the agency had few good remedies available to it.[17] The acquired hospital, Community, already had been converted to a skilled nursing/rehabilitative care facility. Thus, the effects of the merger could have been reversed only at considerable cost. Further, Sutter Health, a major Northern California hospital chain, had announced plans to construct an acute care hospital in Santa Cruz, and had already purchased a 3.8

---

[16] (...continued)
Issuance of Consent Order *In the Matter of Dominican Santa Cruz Hospital, et al.* 188 F.T.C. 382 (1994).

[17] *See* Statements of Chairman Steiger, Commissioner Azcuenaga, and Commissioner Yao *In the Matter of Dominican Santa Cruz Hospital, et al.* 118 F.T.C. 382 (1994).

acre site toward that end.[18] The FTC reasoned that entry by this entity likely would already have occurred by the time divestiture could be completed, thereby moving the market closer to the pre-merger status quo more rapidly than could be accomplished through the FTC's administrative process.[19] As it turned out, some time in the second quarter of 1996, Sutter Health opened the Sutter Maternity and Surgery Center with 30 licensed and 21 staffed beds.

IV. Methods and Data

A. The Empirical Model

To identify the equilibrium price effects of the Dominican/Santa Cruz acquisition, we employ an empirical specification that borrows elements from Schumann *et al.* (1992) and Barton and Sherman (1984). Like Schumann *et al.*, we estimate the reduced form equation for price:

$$P_{it} = P(W_{it}, Z_{it}, M_t)$$

---

[18] *Sacramento Business Journal*, March 16, 1992.

[19] "Sutter Health, a major Northern California hospital chain, announced plans to construct an acute care hospital in Santa Cruz, which would restore a third hospital competitor in the market. The very real prospect that Sutter will enter this market, before a divestiture decree could be obtained through litigation and a willing buyer found, is an additional factor weighing against pursuit of a divestiture order." *See* Statement of Chairman Janet D. Steiger in Support of Final Issuance of Consent Order *In the Matter of Santa Cruz Hospital, et al.* 188 F.T.C. 382 (1994).

where P_{it} is the price of hospital i at time t; Z_{it} is a vector of demand shifters (*e.g.*, income); W_{it} is a vector of input prices; and M_t is a dummy variable set equal to one for all time periods subsequent to the transaction. In section V, below, we estimate equation [1] separately for Dominican Hospital and its closest remaining rival, Watsonville Hospital.

Because we cannot observe all of the exogenous factors that might affect the equilibrium prices of the merged entity and its competitors, we incorporate elements of the approach used by Barton and Sherman (1984) and Kim and Singal (1993) in their merger studies. Essentially, these authors analyzed movements in the price of the product affected by the merger, conditional on the price of a substitute product that faces similar demand and cost conditions, but which is unaffected by the merger. In other words, this other product serves as a control group; it is assumed that the exogenous determinants of price (*e.g.*, input prices) affect the "control group" and the "treatment group" equally.[20] If true, and if the merger had no impact on equilibrium price, then the relationship of the price of the merged entity to the price of the "control" would be unchanged post-merger. Post-merger changes in this ratio can then be imputed entirely to the transaction.

As noted earlier, the assumption that exogenous factors affect the merged entity and the control group equally is restrictive – it is unlikely that all of the determinants of

---

[20] *See* note 13, above.

price will be matched across the two groups. Accordingly, we include as regressors, in addition to the price of the control group, the observable determinants of that price (*e.g.,* factor prices faced by the peer group hospitals). This specification avoids the unnecessarily restrictive assumption that all intertemporal differences in the covariance of the two prices is attributable to the change in market structure. Below, the criteria used to construct this control group (which we refer to as the "peer group") are discussed in greater detail.

Carrying out the analysis via the estimation of equation [1] eliminates the necessity of specifying a geographic market for the outputs produced by the merging hospitals. If the Dominican-Community merger was anticompetitive, then the coefficient on the merger dummy variable should be positive,[21] irrespective of the dimensions of the market in which Dominican and Community competed prior to merger.[22] Conversely, if the merger was not anticompetitive, for whatever reason (*e.g.,* low concentration in the relevant market, subsequent entry, offsetting efficiencies, or not-for-profit status), then the coefficient on this variable should be zero (or negative, if

---

[21] As we discuss below, a positive coefficient potentially is also consistent with post-merger quality improvements.

[22] Knowing the dimensions of the market would be important if the merger was anticompetitive, and if we wished to estimate the welfare loss associated with the transaction. Then, we would also wish to know which other hospitals also raised their prices (and by how much). This paper attempts to address a much simpler question: did the merged entity (and its closest rival) raise price post-merger?

merger-related efficiencies reduced costs and prices). In neither case need we specify a geographic market.

B. *Description of the Variables*

1. *Price*

Each calendar quarter, California-licensed hospitals file a Financial Data Report with the Office of Statewide Health Planning and Development (OSHPD). These data allow us to calculate quarterly observations (for 1986 through 1996, inclusive) of the average net revenue received per inpatient acute-care admission for privately insured patients.[23] Of course, hospitals provide numerous inpatient services, some of which

---

[23] In the OSHPD data, there are various categories for both gross and net patient revenue. Net revenue is equal to a hospital's gross revenue minus any discounts that it offers. In the data, the *gross* revenue figures distinguish between inpatient and outpatient revenue, however, the *net* revenue figures do not. As noted by Dranove *et al.* (1993), failure to account for discounts seriously understates the effect of competition on price. Thus, several adjustments must be done in order to obtain estimates of net inpatient revenue from the gross inpatient data. While OSHPD has been collecting quarterly data from hospitals since approximately 1980, data prior to 1986 did not in any way distinguish revenue by payer group. As a result, observations from prior to 1986 were eliminated. For data from 1986 to 1992, net inpatient price was calculated by multiplying total net revenues from non-Medicare, non-Medicaid patients by the ratio of gross *inpatient* revenue to gross *total* revenue at the hospital. While this net revenue figure eliminates Medicare and Medicaid patients it does include revenue from some patients in various non-Medicaid indigent programs. This net revenue figure is then divided by discharges to obtain the average price paid per non-Medicare, non-Medicaid acute-care inpatient. We also adjusted the number of discharges by the ratio (total revenue-bad debt)/total revenue in order to account for bad debt.

For data after 1992, patient revenue for various indigent programs is reported in a separate category. In order to keep the observations consistent over time, revenue from this category was added to the revenue figures for commercially insured patients.

(continued...)

may or may not be demand- or supply-side substitutes. Nevertheless, a single measure of inpatient price is consistent with the so-called "cluster" approach to defining hospital product markets used in virtually all hospital merger investigations.[24]

2. Control Variables

As is obvious, the unit of output employed in this study – an inpatient discharge – is nonhomogeneous. Patient stays can and do vary substantially in terms of their resource intensity. Consequently, cross-sectional and intertemporal comparisons of the "price" of this output are meaningless unless one controls somehow for this heterogeneity.

We employ several such controls. First, like other researchers (*e.g.*, Simpson and Shin (1998)), we construct an index of hospital "casemix." The Healthcare Financing Administration (HCFA) assigns a "caseweight" to each diagnostic related group (DRG).[25] This index measures the "resource intensity," used, on average, for each DRG relative to other DRGs and over time. The OSHPD discharge data set includes the date

---

[23] (...continued)
Net price was then calculated using the same methodology as outlined for the 1986 to 1992 data.

[24] For a critical overview of the "acute care inpatient" product market definition used in hospital merger investigations, see Sacher and Silvia (1998).

[25] DRGs refer to a system of classifying patients based on medical diagnoses and surgical procedures. Originating at Yale University during the 1970s, the DRG system has been widely adopted by payers and providers as a way of classifying patients.

of discharge and DRG for each patient. Using these data, we created a quarterly

casemix indicator for each hospital used in the empirical analysis. This was done as

follows. Each non-Medicare/non-Medicaid discharge at each hospital for each quarter

was weighted using the HCFA caseweight index for the relevant DRG. The weighted

discharges were then summed and divided by the total number of discharges for each

quarter at each hospital to obtain the casemix index.

As a further control for discharge heterogeneity, we also include the average

length-of-stay for privately insured patients. The rationale for including this measure is

straightforward – each additional day of hospitalization requires the consumption of

additional labor and material resources. One cannot compare the price of a discharge

across different time periods, or across different hospitals, unless one controls for

variations in length-of-stay.

Equilibrium hospital prices also will be affected by exogenous changes in factor

prices. We include two variables to control for these shifts. First, HCFA computes a

wage index for all urban areas (a county or set of counties) based on the salaries and

wages of various health care workers in the relevant locale.[26] This index is used to

adjust hospital payments under the Prospective Payment System (PPS) for Medicare.

_____

[26] All hospitals in our "peer group" were located in an MSA for which HCFA creates a wage index. The exception is El Centro Regional Medical Center in Imperial County. For this hospital we used a composite HCFA wage index for non-metropolitan areas of California.

As an additional control variable, we include the BLS Producer Price Index for surgical and medical instruments and apparatus.

It is well-established empirically that the growth of managed care institutions (*e.g.,* HMOs, PPOs) has facilitated more intense price competition among hospitals(*e.g.,* Dranove, Shanley, and White (1993); Kralewski *et al.* (1992)), as well as greater productive efficiency. Consequently, other things equal, we would expect to observe lower prices in markets where selective contracting by managed care organizations is more prevalent. Ideally, we would like to utilize some measure of the market share of managed care institutions in the relevant market. Unfortunately, such data are not readily available. As a proxy, we calculate for each hospital the percentage of total discharges for which the expected payment source is an HMO or other prepaid health plan.

We also control for the effects of the October 1989 northern California earthquake, which inflicted some damage on Watsonville Hospital, and may have reduced (exogenously) Watsonville's productive capacity, leading to higher prices for reasons unrelated to the Dominican transaction.[27] To capture the competitive effects of

---

[27] Though Watsonville Hospital suffered damage from the earthquake, the OSHPAD data provide little support for the proposition that its productive capacity was substantively impaired by this damage. Whether measured by total patient days or total discharges, the OSHPAD data suggest that Watsonville's output actually increased after the quake. A regression of total patient days against a time trend and the **quake** dummy (=1 for 3rd quarter 1989 and afterwards) yields a coefficient on **quake** of 1069.83 (t=3.26). A similar regression using total discharges yields a coefficient (t-statistic) on **quake** equal to 22.03 (0.22).

this event, we create a dummy variable (**quake**) equal to 1 for the 3rd quarter of 1989 and all subsequent periods, and 0 otherwise.

Last, similar to other empirical studies of hospital mergers (*e.g.,* Lynk (1995), Simpson and Shin (1998)), we include a number of other variables to control for exogenous demand- and cost-side variation. These consist of per capita income, the county-level unemployment rate, county population density, share of admissions Medicare, and share of admissions MediCal.

Table 1 contains descriptive statistics for the variables used in empirical analysis.

C. Creation of the Peer Group

As noted above, an important element of our study is the creation of a group of hospitals comparable to Dominican Santa Cruz and other in-market hospitals, and the inclusion of their prices (and the exogenous determinants of their prices) as an explanatory variable in the price equation. By so doing, we hope to control for otherwise unobserved demand and cost factors, unrelated to the merger, that might influence intertemporal price behavior at the merging hospitals. The State of California has undertaken two studies to categorize hospitals into peer groups for purposes of setting Medi-Cal reimbursement levels, the most recent in 1991 (Department of Health Services, 1991).

These studies form the basis for the construction of the peer group used here. The peer grouping method used by the State of California first placed specialty, teaching, and prepaid hospitals in their own separate peer groups. The study then used "cluster" analysis to group rural hospitals and other "unusual" hospitals (*see* State of California (1991), § 5). After the latter were classified into these peer groups, only urban short term facilities remained. These facilities were then subdivided into peer groups on the basis of licensed bed size. In the 1982 study, Dominican Santa Cruz and Community Hospital of Santa Cruz were placed in the "moderately-sized" urban category, while Watsonville was placed in the "small-urban" hospital peer group. In the 1991 study, Dominican Santa Cruz was placed in the "medium-sized urban" hospital peer group, which consisted of all hospitals not elsewhere classified with between 170 and 270 licensed beds. Watsonville was placed in the "moderately small-sized" urban hospital peer group, which consisted of all hospitals not elsewhere classified with between 95 and 170 licensed beds.

We used the following procedure to establish a peer group for the current study. First, to ensure that peer hospitals were located in markets as similar as possible to the Santa Cruz market, hospitals located in counties that were part of very large Primary Metropolitan Statistical Areas (PMSAs) were eliminated. This eliminated hospitals located in the following counties: Los Angeles, Orange, Ventura, Riverside, San Bernardino, San Diego, San Francisco, Alameda, Contra Costa, Marin, San Mateo and

Santa Clara. The competitive environment in such large urbanized areas likely is very different from that found in the less urbanized area of Santa Cruz.

Next, the peer group was restricted to those hospitals that were placed in any of the short term urban hospital peer groups in the 1991 California study, and were licensed with between 100 and 300 beds in that year. While somewhat arbitrary, these licensed bed cut-offs would appear to limit the sample to hospitals reasonably comparable to the hospitals in Santa Cruz. This left 41 potential peer group hospitals. We next eliminated those hospitals in this group that were not between 100 and 300 licensed beds, and/or did not fall under one of the urban hospital groupings in the 1982 California Peer Group survey. This left 33 potential peer group hospitals. We next eliminated any hospitals that did not report between 100 and 300 beds in the 1996 *AHA Guide*. This left 25 potential peer group hospitals. We then eliminated all hospitals that had themselves been involved in a horizontal acquisition as reported in the OSHPD Hospital History Listing database. This group of 17 remaining hospitals comprise our peer group (*see* Appendix A).

V.   Empirical Results

Tables 2 and 3 present the estimated parameters of the reduced form price equation. Table 2 contains the results for Dominican; Table 3 presents the results for Watsonville.[28] The parameters are estimated using ordinary least squares; autocorrelation and heteroskedasticity consistent standard errors are computed using the Newey-West (1987) estimator.[29] These results are consistent with the possibility that the merger was anticompetitive.

---

[28] We conducted a Chow test to determine if the Watsonville and Dominican data should be pooled. The Chow test rejected this restriction at the 5 percent significance level. Accordingly, we estimate the price equation separately for each hospital.

[29] *See* Newey and West (1987) and Greene (1997, p. 506). The Newey-West estimator is a refinement of the White (1980) heteroskedasticity-consistent estimator; it produces standard errors that consistently estimate the true covariance estimator without requiring the researcher to specify the precise structure of the covariance matrix. The Newey-West estimator does require the researcher to specify the maximum length of the autocorrelation relationship; we experimented with lags of 1, 2, and 3. For the Dominican equation, the corresponding t-statistics on the **merge** dummy ranged in value from 1.986 (lag=1) to 2.47 (lag=3).

We also estimated the parameters of these equations using OLS and feasible GLS using the Hildreth-Lu correction for first-order autocorrelation. These results are similar to those reported in Tables 2 and 3; the principal difference is found in the Watsonville equation, where the statistical significance of the coefficient on **merge** fell. In the Dominican price equation, the estimated coefficients (t-statistics) on **merge** were: 1153.6 (2.44) [OLS]; 1300.6 (2.66) [Hildreth-Lu]. In the Watsonville equation, the estimated coefficients (t-statistics) on **merge** were: 497.5 (0.73) [OLS]; 550.6 (0.81) [Hildreth-Lu].

The results in Table 2 present the strongest evidence of an anticompetitive post-merger price increase. In column (a), which presents the fully specified version of the equation, the coefficient on **merge**, the merger dummy variable, suggests a substantial post-merger price increase – over $1,000 per admission, which represents a price increase of approximately 30 percent (Dominican's pre-merger average real revenue per admission was approximately $3,700). Most of the other coefficients in this equation are statistically insignificant – the only exceptions are Dominican's average length-of-stay (**length-of-stay_d**), which has the expected positive coefficient, and the Producer Price Index for surgical and medical instruments (**ppi_med**), which also has the expected positive coefficient.[30]

The finding of a post-merger price increase at Dominican is weakened, though not eliminated, by imposing restrictions on the reduced form equation. In column (b) of Table 2, we drop the **quake** dummy variable from the equation. In column (c), we further restrict the peer group variables to have zero coefficients. As can be seen, these restrictions cause the magnitude of the coefficient on **merge** to fall. Even in the most restricted version of the equation (*i.e.,* column (c)), however, the results indicate that the merger raised price per admission by about $700. In this specification, the hypothesis

---

[30] We also estimate this equation using the log of the ratio of the Dominican (Watsonville) price to the average peer group price. The basic results are unchanged.

that the true value of this parameter equals zero is rejected at the p = .18 significance

level.[31]

Table 3 presents the estimated coefficients for the Watsonville price equation.

The pattern of results is similar to that for Dominican. Most importantly, the coefficient

on **merge** in the Watsonville equation suggests a post-merger price increase, albeit of a

smaller economic magnitude (approximately one-half as large) than the estimated

increase at Dominican, and of a lesser degree of statistical significance.[32] This finding --

a smaller, but positive price effect -- is consistent with the predictions of many

differentiated products oligopoly models,[33] and is particularly noteworthy, given that

Watsonville is the type of hospital – namely, locally sponsored and administered –

hypothesized to be least likely to exercise market power.

---

[31] We test the null hypothesis that the parameters on the peer group variables jointly equal zero. For the Dominican equation, the test statistic (distributed $F_{(10, 19)}$) equals 1.14, which means that the null hypothesis can be rejected only at p=.39. For the Watsonville equation, the corresponding test statistic and significance level are 1.23 (p=.33).

[32] We can reject the null hypothesis that the true parameter on **merge** equals zero at the 31 percent level in the unrestricted version of the equation (*see* Table 3, column (a)). Columns (b) and (c) of Table 3 present restricted versions of the Watsonville price equation. Comparing the coefficients on **merge** across these different specifications shows that the estimated price effect of the transaction on Watsonville's price is fairly robust – it remains at about $500 per admission. The statistical significance of this coefficient increases as these restrictions are imposed -- from p = .31 in column (a) to p = .16 in column (c).

[33] *See, e.g.,* Werden and Froeb (1994, p. 413). Werden and Froeb analyze the competitive consequences of horizontal mergers in differentiated products markets where firms engage in static price competition.

While the empirical results presented in Tables 2 and 3 are consistent with an anticompetitive post-merger price increase, our inability to observe and measure quality perfectly means that we cannot rule out the possibility that the price increases reflect improvements in quality, rather than increased price-cost markups with unchanged (or even diminished) quality levels. We are, however, skeptical about the validity of this interpretation. First and foremost, the parties to the acquisition made no such claims in defense of the transaction. Rather, the parties claimed that the efficiencies from the transaction would derive from the realization of scale-related production efficiencies.[34] To the extent that such scale economies were realized, we would expect prices to fall, other things held constant.

It is perhaps conceivable that consolidation of particular services at Dominican could lead to volume-related quality increases – for example, because clinical outcomes for some procedures improve as the procedure is performed with higher frequency at a particular location.[35] Then, Dominican might be able to capture some or all of the value of this quality increase in the form of higher prices.

_____

[34] *See* Statement of Commissioner Yao. Dominican claimed that Community Hospital was inefficiently small, and that efficiencies could therefore be realized by converting it to a skilled nursing/rehabilitation facility, and channeling its patients to Dominican.

[35] For a large number of clinical procedures there is empirical evidence that outcomes improve with patient volume. *See, e.g.,* Begg *et al.* (1998) and Selby *et al.* (1996).

The problem with this explanation is that it fails to explain the post-merger increase in price at Watsonville Hospital. If the elimination of Community Hospital as a provider of the services in question leads to higher (quality-unadjusted) prices at Dominican because of the efficiencies described in the preceding paragraph, Watsonville would either have to (1) cut its price (assuming that its quality remained unchanged); or (2) somehow try to match Dominican's quality increase. If Watsonville captured some of the patient flow that otherwise would have patronized Community, then it too might be able to realize volume-related quality increases. But if this occurred, then it is unclear why prices would rise unless the transaction also had competitive effects.[36] In a competitive market, prices are determined by cost, not demand (demand determines the equilibrium quantity, but price will be determined by marginal cost). If the quality of certain services increases at both hospitals (but costs remain unchanged), then there will be a market-wide increase in demand for the service, leading to an increase in the total quantity sold. But if marginal costs are constant, and prices are determined competitively, the price at which this service is sold would not change. If prices increase, it suggests that the transaction has increased market power, even if it simultaneously yielded efficiencies.

---

[36] The other possibility is that marginal cost increases with output. This possibility is difficult to reconcile with the efficiency claims actually put forth by the parties; *i.e.*, that the merger allowed the merged entity to enjoy scale-related reductions in unit cost.

It perhaps is conceivable that the merger led to other types of quality increases at both Dominican and Watsonville that are not related to volume, but which manifest themselves in greater resource use per patient. If so, we might observe an increase in expenses per admission post-merger -- hence prices -- at both hospitals, other things held constant. We carry out two tests of this hypothesis. First, in Tables 4 and 5 we regress real expenses per inpatient admission against the same explanatory variables employed in the regressions contained in Tables 2 and 3. We find little evidence that the merger resulted in greater average expenses. Compared to the coefficients on the **merge** dummy in the price equations, the corresponding coefficients in Tables 4 and 5 are small in magnitude, and never differ from zero at conventional levels of statistical significance.

We conduct a second test of this efficiency hypothesis by examining data on patient flows. If the transaction improved the quality of hospital care provided in Santa Cruz County, we would expect to observe (*ceteris paribus*) a reduction in the proportion of Santa Cruz County residents who seek hospital care outside of the county. That is, we would expect to observe an increase in the Elzinga-Hogarty "little in from outside" ("LIFO") statistic.[37] For a given year, the LIFO statistic equals the total number of patients admitted at Santa Cruz hospitals who were Santa Cruz County residents, divided by the total number of Santa Cruz county residents admitted at *any* hospital (*i.e.,* whether at a Santa Cruz County hospital or elsewhere). To test the efficiency

---

[37] Elzinga and Hogarty (1973).

hypothesis, we regress the LIFO statistic against a constant and the **merge** dummy. If the efficiency hypothesis is correct, we would expect to obtain a positive coefficient on **merge**. As it turns out, however, the coefficient is negative and statistically insignificant.[38] Thus, this result also fails to support the efficiency hypothesis.

Two other aspects of these empirical findings merit comment. First, we observe that the coefficient on **entry** (the dummy variable set equal to one for those time periods after the entry of the Sutter mini-hospital) was not consistently negative across specifications (*e.g.*, compare Table 2 to Table 3), as theory would predict, and was never different from zero at conventional significance levels. As noted earlier, the FTC's rationale for not pursuing a divestiture remedy in this matter was predicated in part on the decision of Sutter to enter this market.[39] It now appears that the FTC overestimated the competitive impact of this entry. This error probably was attributable to the limited scale and scope at which entry actually occurred. The new hospital was not a full-scale acute care institution, but rather a very small (21 staffed beds) maternity and surgery center. It is implausible that this institution would impose the same competitive constraints on incumbent producers as did Community hospital.[40]

---

[38] The estimated regression is: LIFO =.6881 - .0097***merge** + e.
$$(77.42) \quad (-0.87)$$
T-statistics are in parentheses.

[39] *See* note 19, above.

[40] As noted earlier (*see* note 34, above), Dominican had argued that Community (180 beds) was inefficiently small. If true, then it surely follows that a 21 bed hospital is
(continued...)

30

VI.   Conclusion

The combination of Dominican Hospital and Community in Santa Cruz, California, affords researchers a rare opportunity to study the competitive effects of a horizontal merger in a concentrated antitrust market dominated by not-for-profit producers. We have attempted to assess these effects by estimating a reduced form price equation for the merged entity and its closest rival, Watsonville Community Hospital. Controlling for casemix, input prices, and other cost- and demand-side characteristics, our results suggest that both hospitals raised prices in the aftermath of the transaction. The small scale entry that occurred after the merger was consummated did not mitigate this price increase. These price increases -- and in particular, the price increase at Watsonville hospital, a locally-sponsored and administered community hospital -- suggest strongly that mergers involving not-for-profit hospitals are a legitimate focus of antitrust concern. While one cannot rule out unequivocally the possibility that this price increase reflects some unmeasured increase in hospital quality, a more plausible interpretation is that the merger created market power that allowed Dominican and Watsonville to increase price-cost markups.

---

[40] (...continued)
too small to provide efficiently the full range of services necessary to compete with Dominican.

Table 1

Descriptive Statistics

Variable Name	Description	Mean	Minimum	Maximum
rprice_d	real net revenue per admission, Dominican Hospital	4434.55	3212.89	5882
rprice_w	real net revenue per admission, Watsonville Hospital	3897.98	1794.32	6490.128
rprice_p	real net revenue per admission, peer group hospitals	4955.76	3454.33	6091.85
length-of-stay_d	average length-of-stay, Dominican Hospital	4.01	2.71	5.63
length-of-stay_w	average length-of-stay, Watsonville Hospital	3.99	2.71	6.79
length-of-stay_p	average length-of-stay, peer group hospitals	4.38	3.70	4.93
medi-Cal share_d	share of admissions MediCal, Dominican Hospital	0.14	0.051	0.17
medi-Cal share_w	share of admissions MediCal, Watsonville Hospital	0.29	0.10	0.48

Variable Name	Description	Mean	Minimum	Maximum
medi-Cal share_p	share of admissions MediCal, peer group hospitals	0.21	0.17	0.24
medicare share_d	share of admissions Medicare, Dominican Hospital	0.39	0.33	0.44
medicare share_w	share of admissions Medicare, Watsonville Hospital	0.31	0.22	0.40
medicare share_p	share of admissions Medicare, peer group hospitals	0.38	0.34	0.40
casemix_d	casemix index, Dominican	0.85	0.75	1.04
casemix_w	casemix index, Watsonville	0.76	0.67	0.87
casemix_p	casemix index, peer group hospitals	0.94	0.84	1.05
density_p	population density, peer group counties	101.43	89.97	110.07
density_s	population density, Santa Cruz County	516.96	486.10	539.57
hmo_d	share of admissions HMO insured, Dominican	0.25	0	0.50

33

Variable Name	Description	Mean	Minimum	Maximum
hmo_w	share of admissions HMO insured, Watsonville	0.06	0	0.25
hmo_p	share of admissions HMO insured, peer group	0.15	0.06	0.23
income_s	real per capita income, Santa Cruz County	16104.97	14464.69	17700.51
income_p	real per capita income, peer group counties	13253.29	12968.84	13703.24
ppi_med	producer price index, medical & surgical instruments	121.19	107.27	131.27
unemploy_p	unemployment rate, peer group counties	10.53	8.16	14.40
unemploy_s	unemployment rate, Santa Cruz County	8.35	5.37	13.83
merge	= 1 for quarters after merger occurred	0.6304348	0	1
entry	= 1 for quarters after entry occurred	0.1086957	0	1
run_qtr	time trend	23.54348	1	48

Variable Name	Description	Mean	Minimum	Maximum
run_qtr2	time trend squared	732.5435	1	2304
wage_d	HCFA wage index, Dominican	1.22	0.97	1.42
wage_w	HCFA wage index, Watsonville	1.20	0.97	1.39
wage_p	HCFA wage index, peer group	1.16	1.12	1.24
expadm_d	real expense per admission, Dominican	4118.93	3212.4	4986.1
expadm_w	real expense per admission, Watsonville	3343.72	2582.8	3969.6
expadm_p	real expense per admission, peer hospitals	4038.26	3185.02	4628.92
quake	= 1 for 3rd quarter 1989 and after, 0 otherwise	.70	0	1
merge	= 1 for 2nd quarter 1990 and after, 0 otherwise	.63	0	1
entry	= 1 for 2nd quarter 1996 and after, 0 otherwise	.11	0	1

Table 2

Dominican Hospital Price Regression

Quarterly Data, 1986-96

Dependent Variable = real net revenue per private admission

	Coefficient (t-statistic)	Coefficient (t-statistic)	Coefficient (t-statistic)
merge	1179.92 (1.93)	1153.63 (1.99)	737.46 (1.356)
income_p	-1.25 (-0.74)	-1.26 (-0.78)	
income_s	-0.19 (-0.70)	-.20 (-0.75)	-.25 (-1.57)
density_p	-236.8 (-0.95)	-230.8 (-0.96)	
density_s	47.89 (0.72)	45.59 (0.70)	-9.73 (-0.41)
unemploy_p	-302.19 (-0.81)	-369.82 (-1.04)	
unemploy_s	125.43 (0.68)	156.43 (0.88)	-75.37 (-2.53)
length-of-stay_d	461.66 (2.98)	437.96 (2.96)	469.86 (2.89)
length-of-stay_p	-153.91 (-0.27)	-13.67 (-0.03)	
hmo_d	-284.10 (-0.12)	-448.06 (-.20)	-679.83 (-0.55)
hmo_p	6780.54 (0.55)	6587.93 (0.54)	
casemix_p	-9376.14 (-1.26)	-10185.27 (-1.42)	
casemix_d	1081.09 (0.33)	1125.12 (0.34)	-1524.21 (-0.70)

	Coefficient (t-statistic)	Coefficient (t-statistic)	Coefficient (t-statistic)
wage_p	94.71 (0.01)	926.02 (0.15)	
wage_d	-756.33 (-0.61)	-713.21 (-0.58)	-82.71 (-0.13)
rprice_p	.14 (0.28)	.18 (0.36)	
medicare share_d	1909.25 (0.42)	2625.13 (0.55)	3464.04 (1.37)
medicare share_p	-9161.47 (-0.58)	-11677.03 (-0.76)	
medi-Cal share_d	2410.38 (0.45)	1956.57 (0.37)	1109.31 (0.39)
medi-Cal share_p	-4574.66 (-0.19)	-3710.94 (-0.15)	
ppi_med	253.50 (1.89)	294.69 (3.18)	108.49 (2.16)
run_qtr	-96.75 (-0.60)	-117.87 (-0.78)	26.40 (0.27)
run_qtr2	0.78 (0.40)	1.03 (0.56)	-0.74 (-0.89)
entry	280.62 (0.39)	257.16 (0.36)	670.12 (2.35)
quake	278.89 (0.63)		
intercept	4634.23 (0.18)	1066.04 (0.04)	-1408.28 (-0.09)
	N = 44 R^2 = .89	N = 44 R^2 = .88	N= 44 R^2 = .84

Newey-West heteroskedasticity and autocorrelation
consistent standard errors (lag length = 1)

Table 3

Watsonville Hospital Price Regression

Quarterly Data, 1986-96

Dependent Variable = real net revenue per private admission

	Coefficient (t-statistic)	Coefficient (t-statistic)	Coefficient (t-statistic)
merge	428.42 (1.48)	497.47 (1.44)	524.30 (1.52)
income_p	-1.44 (-0.58)	-0.83 (-0.34)	
income_s	-0.59 (-1.57)	-0.55 (-1.44)	-.63 (-3.17)
density_p	1.64 (0.01)	91.82 (0.31)	
density_s	-65.57 (-0.62)	-77.70 (-0.77)	-96.15 (-3.35)
unemploy_p	-192.81 (-0.58)	89.83 (0.26)	
unemploy_s	75.96 (0.37)	-68.12 (-0.31)	3.82 (0.07)
length-of-stay_w	661.65 (3.13)	589.53 (2.81)	746.46 (4.24)
length-of-stay_p	1564.40 (1.27)	1082.68 (0.97)	
hmo_w	-3001.02 (-1.27)	-2034.23 (-0.87)	-2926.96 (-1.15)
hmo_p	-2909.30 (-0.19)	-5026.07 (-0.32)	
casemix_p	-1333.34 (-0.14)	1593.00 (0.19)	
casemix_w	6441.82 (1.66)	6738.19 (1.76)	7241.37 (3.38)

	Coefficient (t-statistic)	Coefficient (t-statistic)	Coefficient (t-statistic)
wage_p	3268.53 (0.28)	-1031.73 (-0.10)	
wage_w	-245.38 (-0.11)	92.20 (0.04)	-676.05 (-0.50)
rprice_p	0.02 (0.03)	-0.09 (-0.11)	
medicare share_w	1547.97 (0.32)	3444.37 (-.70)	1220.01 (0.25)
medicare share_p	-22510.47 (-1.47)	-16165.86 (-0.99)	
medi-Cal share_w	-4439.67 (-1.84)	-3690.78 (-1.47)	-3817.34 (-1.91)
medi-Cal share_p	3832.57 (0.11)	-2018.22 (-0.06)	
ppi_med	472.47 (2.48)	279.54 (1.52)	228.73 (2.21)
run_qtr	-108.34 (-0.47)	-25.37 (-.11)	109.46 (0.94)
run_qtr2	0.89 (0.29)	-.22 (-0.07)	-2.03 (-1.43)
entry	-525.84 (-0.93)	-416.75 (-0.66)	25.75 (0.05)
quake	-1023.69 (-1.82)		
intercept	4964.34 (0.14)	16107.88 (0.48)	27732.12 (1.42)
	N = 44 R^2 = .88	N = 44 R^2 = .87	N = 44 R^2 = .84

Newey-West heteroskedasticity and autocorrelation
consistent standard errors (lag length = 1)

Table 4

Dominican Hospital Expense Regression

Quarterly Data, 1986-96

Dependent Variable = real inpatient expenses per admission

	Coefficient (t-statistic)	Coefficient (t-statistic)	Coefficient (t-statistic)
merge	143.94 (1.02)	110.41 (0.83)	84.87 (0.66)
income_p	.22 (0.21)	0.24 (0.21)	
income_s	-0.27 (-1.62)	-0.28 (-1.63)	-0.24 (-3.93)
density_p	-9.94 (-0.07)	-6.02 (-0.04)	
density_s	3.38 (0.09)	-0.54 (-0.01)	-14.30 (-1.84)
unemploy_p	19.05 (0.13)	-53.27 (-0.37)	
unemploy_s	-25.51 (-0.32)	6.61 (0.08)	-15.64 (-0.79)
length-of-stay_d	7.34 (0.13)	-16.65 (-0.25)	-58.95 (-0.71)
length-of-stay_p	197.67 (0.76)	369.77 (1.37)	
hmo_d	-828.36 (-0.70)	-1003.58 (-0.87)	-417.71 (-0.76)
hmo_p	-1170.30 (-0.32)	-1122.31 (-0.32)	
casemix_p	-644.95 (-0.24)	-1527.72 (-0.49)	
casemix_d	311.36 (0.30)	308.32 (0.28)	-238.12 (-0.27)

	Coefficient (t-statistic)	Coefficient (t-statistic)	Coefficient (t-statistic)
wage_p	4986.65 (1.69)	5853.47 (1.84)	
wage_d	-491.62 (-1.30)	-466.61 (-1.23)	294.96 (1.17)
expense_p	0.27 (0.56)	0.29 (0.61)	
medicare share_d	735.17 (0.44)	1438.33 (0.82)	780.20 (0.47)
medicare share_p	1082.31 (0.18)	-1341.07 (-0.23)	
medi-Cal share_d	1609.24 (0.49)	1045.77 (0.33)	395.13 (0.26)
medi-Cal share_p	-6820.35 (-1.17)	-1341.07 (-0.23)	
ppi_med	-46.42 (-0.67)	-0.13 (-0.002)	22.78 (0.81)
run_qtr	138.48 (1.54)	120.37 (1.36)	80.30 (2.94)
run_qtr2	-1.15 (-1.04)	-0.93 (-0.82)	-0.78 (-2.34)
entry	341.79 (1.14)	323.94 (1.11)	419.14 (2.68)
quake	308.11 (1.70)		
intercept	1780.65 (0.15)	-1707.39 (-0.17)	11244.89 (2.76)
	N = 44 R^2 = .96	N = 44 R^2 = .96	N = 44 R^2 = .94

Newey-West heteroskedasticity and autocorrelation
consistent standard errors (lag length = 1)

Table 4

Watsonville Hospital Expense Regression

Quarterly Data, 1986-96

Dependent Variable = real inpatient expenses per admission

	Coefficient (t-statistic)	Coefficient (t-statistic)	Coefficient (t-statistic)
merge	123.47 (0.60)	121.37 (0.62)	155.93 (0.72)
income_p	-0.93 (-0.90)	-0.95 (-0.95)	
income_s	-0.15 (-0.81)	-0.15 (-0.82)	-0.32 (-3.76)
density_p	63.92 (0.43)	61.4 (0.44)	
density_s	-2.58 (-0.07)	-2.32 (-0.06)	-34.23 (-2.86)
unemploy_p	151.03 (0.59)	143.26 (0.62)	
unemploy_s	-66.13 (-.044)	-62.28 (-0.45)	14.56 (0.50)
length-of-stay_w	223.34 (2.12)	225.21 (2.16)	240.91 (5.54)
length-of-stay_p	-573.39 (-1.30)	-559.09 (-1.41)	
hmo_w	174.69 (0.09)	148.52 (0.08)	-0.67 (0.00)
hmo_p	-8915.0 (-1.64)	-8837.91 (-1.72)	
casemix_p	1865.20 (0.52)	1785.43 (0.55)	
casemix_w	-793.64 (-0.52)	-805.12 (-0.53)	-919.8 (-0.83)

	Coefficient (t-statistic)	Coefficient (t-statistic)	Coefficient (t-statistic)
wage_p	-1061.92 (-0.28)	-939.29 (-0.27)	
wage_w	1799.07 (1.76)	1787.93 (1.87)	-170.24 (-0.41)
expense_p	-0.42 (-0.42)	-0.42 (-0.42)	
medicare share_w	4648.03 (1.93)	4597.5 (1.99)	2809.34 (1.73)
medicare share_p	-1914.61 (-0.29)	-2077.00 (-0.32)	
medi-Cal share_w	-329.37 (-0.21)	-348.62 (-0.23)	-1349.59 (-1.38)
medi-Cal share_p	-48.87 (-0.01)	160.19 (0.01)	
ppi_med	-56.90 (-0.68)	-51.61 (-0.71)	-21.18 (-0.36)
run_qtr	83.57 (0.53)	81.47 (0.53)	100.09 (2.17)
run_qtr2	-0.84 (-0.42)	-0.80 (-0.43)	-0.35 (-0.48)
entry	226.26 (0.63)	223.12 (0.64)	-70.75 (-0.49)
quake	27.83 (0.09)		
intercept	19206.04 (1.22)	18897.04 (1.23)	25973.83 (3.71)
	N = 44 R^2 = .84	N = 44 R^2 = .84	N = 44 R^2 = .74

Newey-West heteroskedasticity and autocorrelation
consistent standard errors (lag length = 1)

References

Barro, Jason R. and David M. Cutler, "Consolidation in the Medical Care Marketplace: A Case Study from Massachusetts," *NBER Working Paper* No. 5957, March 1997.

Barton, David M. and Roger Sherman, "The Price and Profit Effects of Horizontal Merger: A Case Study," *Journal of Industrial Economics,* 33 (1984), 165-177.

Begg, Colin B. *et al.* "Impact of Hospital Volume on Operative Mortality for Major Cancer Surgery," *Journal of the American Medical Association* 280 (November 25, 1998), 1747-51.

Bresnahan, Timothy. "Empirical Studies of Industries With Market Power," in Schmalensee and Willig, eds., *Handbook of Industrial Organization, vol. II,* 1989.

Connor, Robert A., Roger D. Feldman, and Bryan E. Dowd, "The Effects of Market Concentration and Horizontal Mergers on Hospital Costs and Prices," *International Journal of the Economics of Business* 5 (1998), 159-80.

Connor, Robert A., Roger D. Feldman, Bryan E. Dowd and Tiffany A. Radcliff, "Which Types of Hospital Mergers Save Consumer Money?," *Health Affairs,* 16 (1997), 62-74.

Department of Health Services, State of California. *Hospital Peer Grouping*, 1991.

Dranove, David, "Pricing by Non-Profit Institutions: The Case of Hospital Cost-Shifting," *Journal of Health Economics,* 7 (1988), 48-49.

Dranove, David, Mark Shanley, and William White, "Price and Concentration in Hospital Markets: The Switch from Patient-Driven to Payer-Driven Competition," *Journal of Law & Economics,* 36 (1993), 179-204.

Eckbo, B. Espen. "Horizontal Mergers, Collusion, and Stockholder Wealth," *Journal of Financial Economics* 11 (1983), 241-73.

Elzinga, Kenneth, and Thomas Hogarty. "The Problem of Geographic Market Definition in Antimerger Suits," *Antitrust Bulletin* 18 (1973), 45-81.

Greene, William. *Econometric Analysis (3rd edition),* 1997.

Joskow, Paul, "The Effects of Competition and Regulation on Hospital Bed Supply and the Reservation Quality of the Hospital," *Bell Journal of Economics,* 11(1980), 421-47.

Keeler, Emett, Glenn Melnick, and Jack Zwanziger, "The Changing Effects of Competition on Non-Profit and For-Profit Hospital Pricing Behavior," *Journal of Health Economics* 18 (1999), 69-86.

Kessler, Daniel, and Mark McClellan, "Designing Hospital Antitrust Policy to Promote Social Welfare," *NBER Working Paper No. 6897*, January 1999.

Kim, E. Han and Vijay Singal, "Mergers and Market Power: Evidence From the Airline Industry," *American Economic Review* 83 (1993), 549-69.

Kralewski, John *et al.*, "Factors Related to the Provision of Hospital Discounts for HMO Inpatients," *Health Services Research* 27 (1992), 133-53.

Lynk, William J. "Nonprofit Hospital Mergers and the Exercise of Market Power," *Journal of Law & Economics,* 38 (1995), 437-461.

MacKinlay, A. Craig. "Event Studies in Economics and Finance," *Journal of Economic Literature* 35 (1997), 13-39.

Manheim, Larry M., Gloria J. Bazzoli, and Min-Woong Sohn, "Local Hospital Competition in Large Market Areas," *Journal of Economics & Management Strategy,* 3 (1994), 143-167.

Melnick, Glenn A., Jack Zwanziger, Anil Bamezai, and Robert Pattison, Robert, "The Effects of Market Structure and Bargaining Position on Hospital Prices," *Journal of Health Economics,* 11 (1992), 217-233.

Newey, Whitney and Kenneth West, "A Simple, Positive Semi-Definite, Heteroskedasticity and Autocorrelation Consistent Covariance Matrix, *Econometrica* 55 (1987), 703-8.

Noether, Monica, "Competition Among Hospitals," *Journal of Health Economics* 7 (1988), 259-84.

Pautler, Paul and Michael Vita, "Hospital Market Structure, Hospital Competition, and Consumer Welfare: What Can the Evidence Tell Us?," *Journal of Contemporary Health Law & Public Policy,* 10 (1994), pp. 117-167.

Robinson, James and Hal Luft, "The Impact of Hospital Market Structure on Patient Volume, Average Length of Stay, and the Cost of Care," *Journal of Health Economics,* 4 (1985), 333-56.

Sacher, Seth and Louis Silvia, "Antitrust Issues in Defining the Product Market for Hospital Services," *International Journal of the Economics of Business,* 5 (1998), 181-202.

Schumann, Laurence, Robert Rogers, and James Reitzes, "Case Studies of the Price Effects of Horizontal Mergers," Federal Trade Commission, *Bureau of Economics Staff Report*, 1992.

_____. "In the Matter of Weyerhauser Company: The Use of a Hold-Separate Order in a Merger With Horizontal and Vertical Effects," *Journal of Regulatory Economics* 11 (1997), 271-89.

Selby, Joe V. *et al.* "Variation Among Hospitals in Coronary-Angiography Practices and Outcomes After Myocardial Infarction in a Large Health Maintenance Organization," *New England Journal of Medicine* (1996), 1888-96.

Simpson, John and Richard Shin, "Do Nonprofit Hospitals Exercise Market Power?," *International Journal of the Economics of Business*, 5 (1988), 141-57.

Sims, Joe. "A New Approach to the Analysis of Hospital Mergers," *Antitrust Bulletin* 64 (1996), 633-48.

Vita, Michael and Laurence Schumann, "The Competitive Effects of Hospital Mergers: A Closer Look," *Journal of Health Economics* 10 (1991), 359-72.

Werden, Gregory, "The Limited Relevance of Patient Migration Data in Market Delineation for Hospital Merger Cases," *Journal of Health Economics* 8 (1989), 363-76.

Werden, Gregory and Luke Froeb. "The Effects of Mergers in Differentiated Products Industries: Logit Demand and Merger Policy," *Journal of Law, Economics, & Organization* 10 (1994), 407-26.

White, Halbert, "A Heteroskedasticity-Consistent Covariance Matrix Estimator and a Direct Test for Heteroskedasticity," *Econometrica* 48 (1980), 817-38.

Wicks, Elliot, Jack Meyer, and Marcia Carlyn, *Assessing the Early Impact of Hospital Mergers*, Economic and Social Research (1998).

Woolley, J. Michael. "The Competitive Effects of Horizontal Mergers in the Hospital Industry," *Journal of Health Economics* 8 (1989), 271-91.

APPENDIX A
PEER GROUP HOSPITALS

HOSPITAL	COUNTY	BEDS-1996
Mercy Hospital*	Kern	261
San Joaquin Community Hospital*	Kern	178
Feather River*	Butte	121
Chico Community Hospital	Butte	105
Oroville*	Butte	120
El Centro	Imperial	107
Natividad	Monterey	181
Salinas Valley	Monterey	180
Queen of the Valley*	Napa	176
Redding Medical Center	Shasta	162
Mercy Medical Center-Redding*	Shasta	220
North Bay Medical Center*	Solano	108
Sutter Solano Medical Center*	Solano	109
Woodland*	Yolo	103
Rideout*	Yuba	128
Marian Medical Center*	Santa Babara	225
Dameron*	San Joaquin	211
*Non-profit hospital